IN SOME QUIET PLACE

IN SOME QUIET PLACE

By Jim Metcalf

Photographs by Sonny Carter

PELICAN PUBLISHING COMPANY

GRETNA 1975

Manufactured in the United States of America

Published by Pelican Publishing Company, Inc.
630 Burmaster Street, Gretna, Louisiana 70053

Library of Congress Cataloging in Publication Data

Metcalf, Jim.
    In Some Quiet Place.
    Poems.
    I. Title.
PS3563.E817I5   811'5.'4   75–16389
ISBN 0–88289–088–3

Contents

IN SOME QUIET PLACE

Some Tomorrow's Morning

On some tomorrow's morning
with sun fair rising,
dawn's pink and yellow fingers
will brush away
the secrets of the night . . .
the mysteries of darkness . . .
    leaving only truth to see,
    the substance of reality.

And I will understand
the meaning of my being,
the me of my existence
and what I am
and why,
    and what I am not
    but ought to be.
And the time of blindness
will be over,
on some tomorrow's morning.
    And I am uncertain.
    I am afraid . . .
Not sure that I can stand
the glare.
Perhaps, I need the darkness
to hide me from the truth!
    to keep me warm and safe
    'neath the blanket
    of my illusions.

The Cookout

The funeral was over, the Missouri skies were gray. The cold wind that swept across the small cemetery was scattering tiny snowflakes. They were banding together now, forming little glaciers in the rough dirt mound that rose above the place where she was buried. She had lived an incredible life, this woman, who as a widow raised a boy and a girl during the depths of the worst depression this nation has ever seen.

She had done alone what two parents often failed to do in those days, and she did it without ever asking for a handout. She did it through hard work, almost any kind she could get. Through determination, through love, and an unbelievable sense of humor . . . this woman who was our mother. She had a way of making good things out of bad ones, a gift that enabled her and us to see something ludicrous in the midst of the worst of crises.

One unbelievably gloomy day in December, when the temperature was below freezing, my sister and I came home from school and found her in an unusually happy frame of mind.

"Guess what we're going to do today?" she asked. "We're going outside and have a wiener roast. We'll gather some wood from the vacant lot next door, build a fire, and have a wiener roast."

We thought it strange with the weather as it was, but we didn't say so. After the fire had been built and the cooking done, we sat for a long time and talked, warmed by the fire and mugs of steaming coffee. When she was certain we were enjoying ourselves, she laughed and told us the real reason for the cookout. The utility company had disconnected our gas service because she couldn't pay the bill. The entire thing had been through necessity but she knew if she had told us, the cookout would have been no fun at all.

10

Her laugh was contagious and even after we had gone to bed for the night, an occasional giggle would echo through the quiet house as we contemplated her benign trickery.

We recalled that incident years later. The day of the funeral, my sister and I relived those few hours of our lives. When we got back to her house, the maid told us that the ice had broken the power lines . . . there was no electricity, no way to prepare dinner. Without saying a word, my sister went to the refrigerator, removed a package of wieners, and headed toward the glass doors that led to the patio.

"We're going to have a wiener roast," she said. "It's just the weather for it."

Our eyes met . . . and we smiled . . . for the first time in weeks . . . we smiled.

Waters of the River

My being
is as the waters of a river;
passing through time and change
and creations of God
and man
that line my way.
Ever changing, ever moving,
pursuing paths
not always of my choosing . . .
traveling at a pace
not always of my heart's desire,
toward some obscure horizon;
some uncertain destiny.

Like the river,
I am moved by powers
I cannot command;
sometimes to linger
in desolate and ugly places
'til I become
a part of what they are . . .
and their look
is on my face . . .
Then suddenly to be swept
past things of beauty,
things of worth,
too fast to grasp . . .
too fast to comprehend.

My life
is as the waters of a river
and I cannot change my course.

Perhaps, there was a time,
somewhere in the beginning,
but not now.
So I will take the path I must
toward whatever seas await me.

Twilight

And now, it dies . . .
this day that was ours
to shape,
to mould,
to make what we wanted it to be.
The darkness soon will steal it,
and it will be ours no more.

But in this death watch
of twilight,
behold, the majesty
of its passing,
and see the tapestry it weaves
and spreads out against the sky . . .
a farewell of gold
and blue on blue . . .
of orange and magenta.

And the rooftops of the city
pose against the backdrop
like actors on a stage,
competing with the grandeur
of the stage they play upon.

And the faceless silhouettes
of people
like shadows without names,
come and go,
oblivious, unseeing,
poorer by a day
than they were at dawn.

Before I Sleep

If I have let
this day pass by
and can't remember
something good about it,
then I have been ungrateful
and I beg forgiveness.

If I have been involved
too much with me ...
my wants and woes,
to see the beauty
that surrounds me,
then I have played the fool
and I am sorry.

If I have not
stretched out my hands
to loved ones
to show them that I care,
then I have been unfeeling
and I am ashamed.

If I have failed to help
when it was needed,
yet asked others to help me
then I have been selfish
and I apologize.

If I have not seen
the face of God
reflected in a million ways
and places,
then I have been blind
and I ask for another chance
to try again
tomorrow.

A Thing of Beauty

I believe in beauty
for beauty's sake,
and that no matter
where it hides,
           it is never wasted.

If, in some dark
and secret place it lies,
where eyes of man
will never see it,
           it is no less lovely.

It needs neither praise
nor adoration
to justify its being.

It exists.
It need do no more
           to serve its purpose.

I believe in beauty
as a noble end
within itself.
And I believe
that God does.

Were it made
for man alone
it would not adorn
the silent floors of oceans
           where he will never walk.

Or be buried for eternity
beneath the sands
          of barren deserts.

If a man should wander
from his charted way
and chance upon
          a thing of beauty, hidden,
then it is he
who will be rewarded;
he who will be changed.

The thing of beauty
will remain the same.
As it was before he came,
so will it be
          when he is gone.

Mister Amigo

She called me "Mr. Amigo." She was fourteen years old when I met her, one of nine children whose parents had come to this country from Mexico shortly after they were married. They had spent their days as migrant farm workers, traveling from one part of the country to another, harvesting the crops of the season. They worked in the fields . . . the parents and the children.

It was during the citrus harvest in the Rio Grande Valley of Texas that I met her—Alicia. She had not been well and was not strong enough to work in the fields, so she was selling newspapers to make her contribution to the family income.

On that first day she barged, unannounced, into my office and blurted, "Paper, friend?"

Already irritated by the fact that I had accomplished absolutely nothing that morning, I blurted back, without even looking up . . . . "You can call me mister," I growled.

"Si," she said. "Mister . . . paper, *Mister* Friend . . . Mister Amigo?"

I looked at her face for the first time. She was smiling. I was stunned by her beauty; her face with eyes so dark, a magnificently delicate nose, and unbelievably white teeth behind her smile.

I shall remember that face always, as I shall remember her. For this child . . . this poorly educated, skinny little girl, changed my entire perspective and taught me much of truth and beauty and the simplicity of both.

She came by my office every day after that. I would buy a paper and for whatever time I could spare, we talked. For every question I would ask, she had an answer, always simple but infinitely meaningful. Once I asked why she was always happy . . . always smiling.

"Because I do things that make God happy," she said. "And when He is happy, He smiles at me and I smile back."

"How do you know what makes Him happy?" I asked.

"I just know," she said. "Everybody knows . . . He tells everybody but they do not always listen."

She talked often about her family and how they traveled from place to place. Once I asked her if they looked forward to a day when they could have a permanent home. She looked at me as though she could not believe the stupidity of the question. Almost indignantly she said, "We have a home now. We live always in each other's hearts and wherever we go, our home is with us. And as long as we are together, it will be so."

One day she walked into my office, and when I saw she was not smiling I knew the day I had dreaded had come. "We are leaving, Mr. Amigo. There is another place . . . another harvest."

Neither of us spoke for a long time. Finally, she leaned over my desk, kissed my cheek, and whispered, "Adios, Mr. Amigo . . . goodbye."

And she was gone. I knew I would never see her again.

Now, when I think back on all of it, I know I must have done something that made God very happy the day He sent her my way. And it was His smile I saw, reflected on Alicia's face.

The Search

I walk alone
in a quiet place.
Searching for the peace
I used to find there;
    but somehow,
        it eludes me.

The sun,
the sky,
the trees,
and the sweetness
of the silence
are all as I recall them.
Yet, there is a restlessness
    within me
        that was not there before.

And I cannot become a part
of the setting
I am in;
and the peace I seek
lies hidden;
perhaps beneath the rubble
    of some dream
        that crumbled,
or some tomb
    of disenchantment
        that took its place.

Perhaps, it no longer
lives at all.
Perhaps, it died
    when youth did . . .
        the day reality was born.

Other Years . . . Other Skies
(Circa 1971) . . . on seeing a flying
demonstration of World War II aircraft.

The years have been most kind to you,
my friends.
You've hardly changed at all
since last we met
at Uxbridge, outside London.
Or was it that old landing strip
between Liège and Brussels?
Or maybe another one,
after that,
in Fritzlar or in Aachen?
The dates, the times,
the sequences,
are not as easily recalled
as once they were;
but it's no matter.
I know we've met before.
I've seen you all
at one time
or another . . .
silhouetted against a contested sky
with death in metal capsules
spilling from your bellies,
or waiting on ramps
in foggy dawns
as lights came on in quonset huts
and young men awoke
from troubled sleep
and faced another day . . .

another nightmare
of reality . . .
then walked slowly to a briefing room
to find out where
it was to happen.
  And when they learned,
   they shrugged
and climbed aboard
and muttered,
"What the hell?
That's as good a place to die
as any."

Yes, I remember
all of you.
How could I forget?
We spent our youth together,
    and shared the dying
       of our innocence
    and the beginning
       of our fear.

The Gift of Love

I have heard men say
the greatest gift of all to give
is the gift of love.
I have heard,
but I do not understand.
I am not sure it is a gift;
a thing
to offer as a present.
I do not believe
there is the power within us
to choose . . . to decide
where our love will go;
to consider possibilities,
then make a list
and add names to it,
or cross them off,
and in the end proclaim:
"To these I will give my love . . .
to these my gift bequeath."

It cannot be so.
For if it were,
there would be no broken hearts,
no songs of love in vain.

It would be such a simple matter
when we received a gift of love,
to be fair
and give ours to the giver
in return;
if we had the power . . .
if we had the choice.

I think we do not give our love;
it is taken from us.
Sometimes by those we want to have it,
by those whose love we've taken;
sometimes by those who take it
without knowing . . .
by those who do not care.

The *ability* to love
is the one true gift.
It is God's gift to all of us;
but He gives us not
the power
to dictate
where it goes.

The Door

When I walk alone
along the streets,
in unfamiliar places,
and see the doors
of houses that line my way,
I think of a house
I used to know,
and a door I lived behind.

A door that last I closed
        in anger,
            a long, long time ago.
And now, I can't remember why.

I only know I never did go back;
though I knew someone inside
            was crying.

I never did go back.
And now, it's too late to try.

A Dream I Overlooked

Now I will be going back;
back to where
my dreams began.

The day I turned,
looked back
and said goodbye,
and walked the path
that led to here
and now,
I thought I'd taken dreams enough
to last a hundred lifetimes.

But now I find that they are gone,
and I don't know where they went . . .
how many died . . .
how many spent . . .
how many realized . . .

I think I must have left
a few behind;
a few I overlooked.

Perhaps they may be there still . . .
somewhere,
in that quiet, untroubled place,
as bright and shiny new
as they were
when I first dreamed them.
So, I'll go back
and look,
and hope
I find just one
to hold
and keep alive,
in the brief and fleeting time
that I have left
for dreaming.

The Teacher

Walk slowly, little one
and let me walk beside you,
as you see the wonders
         you will see.
And I will try to see them
through your eyes . . .
eyes, still fresh
         and beauty seeking;
eyes that do not hide
behind the dimming veil
         of ugliness.

Tell me what you see
         when birds fly by . . .
         when buds of green appear
         on April's trees.
Tell me about the ripples
         on the pond,
         and the colors
         of the flowers.

There is so much
I need to know;
so much I have forgotten.
I remember only
         how to look.
I do not remember
         how to see.
So let me walk along with you
and share the world you know.
         I will be the learner.
         You will be the teacher.

Beauty in the Rain

If you fancy
that you have
an eye for beauty,
    test it
    on a rainy day ...
A cold and foggy day
that wears no make-up.
    Test it
    in the shades of gray
that consume the sun
and rob the flowers
of their colors,
    leaving them forlorn
    in dingy places
like tired and aging ballerinas
in faded dancing clothes;
    huddling in the drafty wings
    of empty opera houses.

Gaze across the rooftops
and the chimneys,
painted
like Utrillo's Paris
on the canvas of the smoke
and fog
of a dying afternoon
in winter.

It takes
no eye for beauty
to find it
on a lovely day.
It thrusts itself upon you
        in the sunshine
        and the warm.

But it hides;
becomes aloof, elusive
        in the cold
        and in the rain.

The Island

In youth,
I dreamed of sailing ships
and voyages
to unknown places.

I dreamed I'd say farewell
to all I knew;
goodbye,
to things familiar.

Then I'd set out to sea
one day
and go where the winds
would blow me;
through storm and calm
and sun and starlight
dancing
on the midnight blue of oceans.

And the wind would sing
its songs to me
and tell me of
          a golden island,
where only peace and beauty were;
A place where I could spend my days
when I grew tired
of roaming.

But the dreams were only
        dreams of youth,
and they, like youth,
have passed me.

And I know if there is
        an isle of gold,
I need not travel far
to find it.
I know if it exists at all,
it is here . . .
        somewhere within me.

My Final Sorrow

The wine of beauty
is all about me
and I cannot drink it all.
I must sip it
slowly
          from small and fragile cups.

For if I tried to have it
all at once
          (as is my first desire to do)
my senses would be dulled,
and I could not know
the magnificence
          of its bouquet.
So I must concentrate
on one majestic,
tiny world
that lives within
the larger one.

I must see the parts
alone
if I am to understand
the whole.
If a sunset I would follow
then the path of setting
I must pursue,
          forgetting that which lies
          outside the direction
                    of my concern.

Yet, I know
if too long I spend
enthralled by a
single wonder,
I will not have time
to see them all
          before the final darkness.

I will have spent my days . . .
and there will be
so much of beauty
I have missed . . .
so much I have not seen.
          And this will be
               my last regret.
          This will be
               my final sorrow.

If You Remember Me

I hope, if you remember me at all,
it will be for what I was,
not for what
you would have had me be,
or what others thought.

I hope that you will say
I knew much of love
and loving,
and dreaming dreams
that stayed alive
as long as I did.

I hope you will not say
that I was strong . . .
or weak . . .
without elaboration.

Say I was weak enough
to cry
when roses died;
to smile when others bloomed
to take their place.

Yet, strong enough
to be unashamed;
to admit
to being gentle.

Say I often walked my path alone
in winter's cold and barren places.
Say I played the loner's role,
but please add,
I was never lonely.

When Summer Dies

September has kissed
the face of a dying Summer,
and the chill winds of Fall
have come again,
breathing life
into a million half-dead memories ...
    of smoke rising
from mounds of leaves
that fell from other trees
in other times
and places ...
    of the wide Summer meadows
of youth,
and days of innocence
and laughter ...
    of the warmth
of a certain lover's breath
in Winter,
beside a fire ...
    of roads and crossroads
    and highways and byways
and people along the way.
And one memory begets another.
They come and go in flashes.
And all the times
and all the places ...
all the feelings,
all the faces
you have ever known
    come back again
    when Summer dies.

The Agreement

They were young and they were in love and they wanted to be married. But there were religious differences and family involvements on both sides and they could see it would never work out . . . it would not be allowed to. So they agreed to see each other no more and they parted. After several weeks, the girl received a letter.

My dearest,

Let me tell you some of the things I have learned about being apart . . . some of the things you must avoid if we are to keep our agreement.

> Don't go to places we used to go.
> I did.
> It was dreadful.
> You'll find they are so much a part of both
> of us that they can never belong to one alone.
> Neither can they be shared with anyone else.
> They were not mine.
> They were not yours.
> They were ours, and they will always be.
> We cannot have them individually.

> Don't do any of the things we used to do.
> Forget the songs we listened to,
> the books we read aloud,
> the windows we looked through
> on rainy days,
> when the world outside was cold
> and we thanked God we had each other.

Forget holidays in the sun,
concerts on Sunday afternoons,
our poets' lines
and midnight wines
and bike trails
through September's red and yellow places.

Forget the breathless way
we threw ourselves at life.
Be sedate.
Be proper.
Change your style and change your hair
and be as far from what you are
as you can be.
And so will I.
And our love will die.
And we will too . . . inside,
but we will keep our bargain.

Winter Sleep

Our unfinished dreams of summer
were kept warm a while
by a kind but aging autumn.
But now,
they are still
and quiet
in a world that belongs to winter.

Gone is our lovely
red and amber season.
And the leaves
that shared with us
the secrets of a sunshine time,
run now before the wind.
        Hurrying, chasing,
            scurrying, racing
to oblivion.
And you are gone
and our dreams are cold.

But I think
they are still alive.
So I will pick them up
and take them back inside
and keep them
somewhere near the fire;
to sleep . . .
to wait along with me
'til April's at the door again . . .
            'til you
            and spring
            come back.

Sing a Song of Silence

Someday, when I can get away
to somewhere where silence is,
I'll while away
a golden day
listening in noiseless bliss.

For the first time in I don't know when
I'll open up my ears and let the quiet in.

I'll walk softly in some grassy place
and not make the faintest trace
of sound waves to vulgarize
my aural paradise.

I want no songs of birds,
no buzz of bees,
no sounds of waves on shore,
no breezes whispering through the trees,
just silence;
nothing more.

I've had enough of noise
to last a thousand lifetimes;
heard it every day
in every way
and throughout most my nighttimes.
Heard bangs and clangs
and screams and shouts . . .
heard booms and zooms
and swearing bouts
and whistles and sirens
and shootin' irons . . . .

Some say the sudden silence
would set my mind awry.
Maybe...
maybe so...
but it's sure as hell worth a try.

A Place I Used to Go

There was a place
I used to go
when I was very young;
when there was no world
quite as real
as the world of books
and make-believe.

Across a meadow,
beneath the trees
that lined a sparkling stream
there was a magic land
where I was king
and others came
by invitation only.

Tom Sawyer used to drop around,
and Huck and Becky Thatcher.
And I remember
one time Tarzan came
and swam up and down the river.

Rupert Brooke and Robert Burns
would come and sit
and write poems
about wars and flowers.

But mostly, I was there alone,
watching the world around me;
and wondering things like
why the sky is blue
and how much a grain of sand
would weigh
if I were an ant.

I wish I could find
that land again;
but I've lost it,
somewhere, in the noise
and hurry.

And I wonder if Tom Sawyer
goes there still . . .
or if he grew old
like I did.

Parade

I look down upon the city
from a high
and silent place,
and watch the little people
walk the tiny streets.

I see them follow
one the other,
forming strange
and changing patterns.

And I wonder
if they know
what they are doing.
        Do they have a reason why?

Or are they marching
to the sound
of madmen
beating drums
in hidden places?

Some Other Time Around

I think we must have loved
before.
Somewhere...
some other time around.
But I cannot recall
the setting
or the years.

I think the part I can remember...
the part
I'm calling *now*
is but a page...
a line or two, perhaps,
from a story that began
a long, long time ago;
when God was younger
and the world was newer
and we played other roles.

And when we turned to darkness,
when we no longer were,
the love we shared
somehow survived
and lived the centuries through.
Then we came back and claimed it
and thought that it was new.

We did not remember
that we had it for our own
before.

We did not know
it had grown stronger
while we were away.

I look at you
and wonder
what other times
we've shared.

I might have seen your face
through midnight fog
at Stonehenge.
Or seen the fires
when Rome burned,
reflected
in your eyes.

But I cannot recall.

I hope that if we meet again
ten thousand years from now,
I will remember
how you look tonight . . .
this moment . . .
just before
I kiss you.

Voices of the Bayous

In whispers quiet,
I hear the voices
from another time
echo through the bayous.
And I listen
to the tales they tell;
of life
and death . . .
of happiness
and sorrow . . .
of men
and boats
and sudden storms
and voyages unfinished.

Where are they now
whose dreams gave life
to wood and steel
and fashioned craft
to reap the harvest
of the water?

Where is he
who homeward came
at sunsets past
and waved to loved ones
waiting on the shore?
And where are they
who watched his face
as he drew near,
knowing the measure of the catch
would be reflected there?
I ask,
Where are they now?

And the voices whisper,
"They are here . . .
and will forever be . . .
in this quiet place . . .
here, beside the water . . . ."

Here and Hereafter

I do not dwell
on thoughts of hell
or heaven.
I love too much
this life ...
this here and now
that God has given me.

I do not need the promise
of some perfect time hereafter
to explain away the questions;
the imperfections of today.

I do not need the threat
of fires eternal
to do whatever good is in me:
for that is born
of love ...
not fear.

And its reward
is love returned;
not in some future life,
but now.

I do not know
how much more
God will give me,
or perhaps, take away.

I do not know
if this life is but a chapter
in a book . . .
or the book itself.

I know only
I will live it
as I will,
no matter
which is true.